SEASONS

Summer

by Mari Schuh

Kaleidoscope
Minneapolis, MN

Where the Quest for Discovery Begins

This edition first published in 2024 by Kaleidoscope Publishing, Inc.

Kaleidoscope Publishing, Inc.
6012 Blue Circle Drive
Minnetonka, MN 55343

Library of Congress Control Number
2023936932

ISBN
978-1-64519-718-8 (library bound)
978-1-64519-766-9 (ebook)

Bigfoot Jr. lurks within one of the images in this book. It's up to you to find him!

Table of Contents

Summer Is Here!

Panya is ready to play at the water park. "It's so hot outside, Grandpa. I can't wait to cool down," she says.

"Yes, it is very hot and **humid**. We are having a summer **heat wave**," Grandpa says.

The **temperature** goes up in summer. Some days are warm. Other days are very hot!

Thunderstorms can form when the weather is warm and humid. Rain and **hail** fall from the clouds. Lightning flashes.

Thunderstorms can have strong winds and lots of rain.

Earth's seasons are spring, summer, fall, and winter. Summer is the warmest season.

FUN FACT
Days are longer in summer.

Summer has more hours of sunlight than winter.

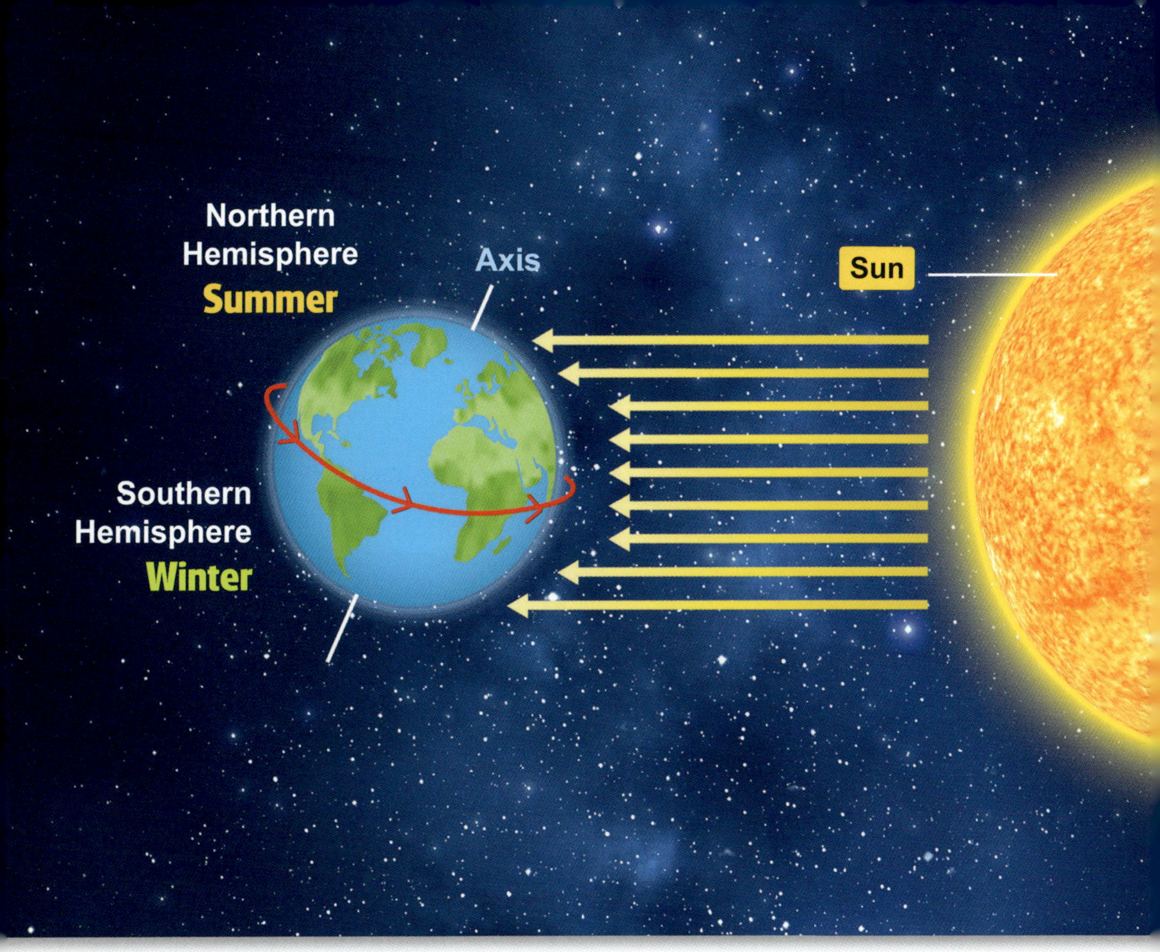

Earth **tilts** as it spins on its **axis**. As Earth travels around the Sun, some areas get more sunlight. When Earth's northern half tilts toward the Sun, it gets more sunlight. Then it is summer on the northern half.

Summer Is Fun!

FUN FACT
There are 300 kinds of watermelon!

People go outside in summer. They play in the park. They have picnics.

People enjoy cold treats in summer. They eat popsicles and ice cream.

Summer is a season of fun. People play sports. They go swimming and hiking too.

Many people
go on vacation
in summer. Some people travel.
Others play at the beach.

What Do People **Use in Summer?**

What do you use in summer?

Animals Are Busy

Red foxes are busy in summer. They hunt for food. They also care for their young.

Summer is the best time to see fireflies glow! The rest of the year, they hide underground.

Crickets are active in summer.
Males chirp loudly.

FUN FACT
Crickets chirp faster in warmer weather.

Deer find **shade** on hot, sunny days. They take a break from the Sun.

Bees bring water droplets into their nest to keep it cool.

Some animals, like elephants, hippos, and pigs, use mud to stay cool.

Turtles sit on sunny rocks. They need heat from the Sun. The Sun warms up their bodies.

Plants in Summer

FUN FACT
Plants need sunlight to make their own food. This process is called photosynthesis.

The Sun shines brightly in summer. Plants grow quickly. People enjoy colorful flowers.

Trees, bushes, and plants grow fruit. People pick apples and peaches. They pick strawberries and blueberries.

"I like your garden, Grandpa. I also liked going to the water park. Can we go again?" Panya asks.

“A thunderstorm is coming. That won’t be good for a trip to the water park. But the rain will be good for my plants!” he says.

Photo Glossary

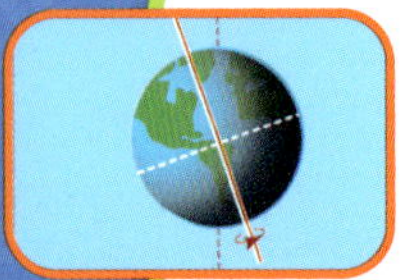

axis: An imaginary line through the center of Earth. Earth spins on its axis. One spin is one day.

hail: Small, round pieces of frozen rain. Hail can be the size of a pea. Some hail is as big as a golf ball.

heat wave: Unusually hot weather that lasts for two or more days. Some heat waves also have humid weather.

humid: Having a lot of water or water vapor in the air. Humid air can feel damp and moist.

shade: An area that is partly dark because light has been blocked off from it. Shaded areas are cooler than sunny areas.

temperature: The measure of how hot or cold something is. A thermometer measures temperature.

thunderstorms: Heavy rainstorms with lightning and thunder. Thunderstorms usually have thick clouds and strong winds.

tilts: Leans, tips, or slants to one side. Earth tilts on its axis.

Read More

Earley, Christina. *In the Summer.* New York, NY: Crabtree Publishing, 2023.

Fraser, Finley. *Summer Weather*. Minneapolis, MN: Bearport Publishing, 2023.

Leaf, Christina. *Summer*. Minneapolis, MN: Bellwether Media, 2023.

Youssef, Jagger. *Seasons*. New York, NY: PowerKids Press, 2023.

Websites

FACTSURFER

Factsurfer.com gives you a safe, fun way to find more information.

1. Go to www.factsurfer.com.
2. Enter "Summer" into the search box and click 🔍
3. Select your book cover to see a list of related websites.

About the Author

Mari Schuh's love of reading began with cereal boxes at the kitchen table. Today she is the author of hundreds of nonfiction books for beginning readers. Mari lives in the Midwest with her husband and their sassy house rabbit. Learn more about her at marischuh.com.

INDEX

PHOTO CREDITS

The images in this book are reproduced through the courtesy of: Lazy_Bear/Shutterstock Images, cover (top left); Cassiohabib/Shutterstock Images, cover (top right); New Africa/Shutterstock Images, cover (bottom); irin-k/Shutterstock Images, title page; Andrei Kuzmik/Shutterstock Images, p. 3; Studio 1One/Shutterstock Images, p. 4; yelantsevv/Shutterstock Images, p. 4–5; Vibrant Image Studio/Shutterstock Images, p. 6; Tomas Ragina/Shutterstock Images, p. 6 (thermometer); Andrey Solovev/Shutterstock Images, p. 7 (circle); Creative Travel Projects/Shutterstock Images, p. 7; Mihai_Andritoiu/Shutterstock Images, p. 8 (all four seasons); Serenko Natalia/Shutterstock Images, p. 10 (top); Rimma Bondarenko/Shutterstock Images, p. 10 (bottom); Max Topchii/Shutterstock Images, p. 11; Sergey Novikov/Shutterstock Images, p. 12 (tops); Sergey Novikov/Shutterstock Images, p. 12 (circle); Mariusz Szczygiel/Shutterstock Images, p. 13 (beach pail); nopparada samrhubsuk/Shutterstock Images, p. 13 (bucket hat); NYS/Shutterstock Images, p. 13 (snorkel, tube, beach ball); New Africa/Shutterstock Images, p. 13 (swimsuit); Bjoern Wylezich/Shutterstock Images, p. 13 (baseball mitt and ball); Cory Woodruff/Shutterstock Images, p. 13 (sunglasses); EM Arts/Shutterstock Images, p. 13 (rubber sandals); alexmisu/Shutterstock Images, p. 13 (water bottle); AB Photographie/Shutterstock Images, p. 14; Fer Gregory/Shutterstock Images, p. 15 (top); Andre Mueller/Shutterstock Images, p. 15 (bottom); Todd Condon Photography/Shutterstock Images, p. 16 (top); Photografiero/Shutterstock Images, p. 16 (bottom); Henk Bogaard/Shutterstock Images, p. 17 (top); David Byron Keener/Shutterstock Images, p. 17 (bottom); PhotographyByMK/Shutterstock Images, p. 18 (top); Zeljko Radojko/Shutterstock Images, p. 18 (bottom); Paradise studio/Shutterstock Images, p. 19 (circle); DenisMArt/Shutterstock Images, p. 19 (blueberries); LightField Studios/Shutterstock Images, p. 20; Paul Maguire/Shutterstock Images, p. 21 (top); Suzanne Tucker/Shutterstock Images, p. 21 (circle); Todd Condon Photography/Shutterstock Images, p. 22 (shade); Ed Connor/Shutterstock Images, p. 22 (heat wave); Creative Travel Projects/Shutterstock Images, p. 22 (thunderstorms); Tomas Ragina/Shutterstock Images, p. 22 (temperature); Suzanne Tucker/Shutterstock Images, p. 22 (hail); matuska/Shutterstock Images, p. 22 (humid); Maks Narodenko/Shutterstock Images, p. 23.